KT-872-066

The royal boil

by Paul Dowswell
illustrated by Chloë March

introducing the oi sound,
as in boy and boil

Royal Princess Joyce had a loyal boyfriend, Floyd.

This fun phonics reader

belongs to

Sarah

DISCARD

Contents

Cover illustration by Chloë March

A catalogue record for this book is available from the British Library

Published by Ladybird Books Ltd
27 Wrights Lane London W8 5TZ
A Penguin Company

2 4 6 8 10 9 7 5 3 1

Tomorrow was their wedding day,
and Joyce was overjoyed.

But Floyd was not a happy boy.
The reason was quite simple.

He had a boil upon his nose —
not just a spot or pimple.

"The guests are sure to point
and laugh, and probably avoid me.

This boil will spoil my wedding
day. It really has annoyed me."

So Floyd made an appointment
to see the royal nurse,

but her poisonous boil ointment
only made the boil worse.

"Your only choice, My Love," said Joyce, "is to grit your teeth and pop it.

Or else, dear boy, the
wedding's off. So do it now...

"or hop it!"

Not now, Brown Cow...

by Richard Dungworth
illustrated by Andy Hammond

introducing the `ow` sound,
as in c**ow** and l**ou**d

"Not so loud, Brown Cow —
I'm off to town now."

When Farmer Brown came back from town, the cows were crowded round.

Megastar Mark

by Lucy Lyes
illustrated by Ken Cox

introducing the **ar** sound,
as in c**a**r

Marcus is the gardener you see working in the park,

smartening up the flower beds
and sweeping up the bark.

But after dark, he's Pop Star Mark, a mega superstar,

with a tartan suit, a sparkling
smile and a supercharged guitar.

Mark's army of fans go barmy when they see their favourite star.

They charge and
barge to touch Mark's arm,
as he gets in his car.

No other artist tops the charts as much as Pop Star Mark.

Number 1

But in daytime, he's just Marcus, brushing leaves up in the park.

phonics

Learn to read with Ladybird

phonics is one strand of Ladybird's **Learn to Read** range. It can be used alongside any other reading programme, and is an ideal way to support the reading work that your child is doing, or about to do, in school.

This chart will help you to pick the right book for your child from Ladybird's three main **Learn to Read** series.

Age	Stage	Phonics	Read with Ladybird	Read it yourself
4-5 years	Starter reader	Books 1-3	Level 1	Level 1
5-6 years	Developing reader	Books 2-9	Level 1-2	Level 2-3
6-7 years	Improving reader	Books 10-12	Level 2-3	Level 3-4
7-8 years	Confident reader		Level 3-4	Level 4

Ladybird has been a leading publisher of reading programmes for the last fifty years. **phonics** combines this experience with the latest research to provide a rapid route to reading success.

...ards

...ds
...oks.

dish

white

This
rhymes
with...

This
rhymes
with...

How to use Book 10

This book introduces your child to the common spellings of the oy, ow and ar sounds. The fun stories will help him* begin reading words including any of the common spelling patterns that represent these sounds.

- Read each story through to your child first. Having a feel for the rhythm, rhyme and meaning of the story will give him confidence when he reads it for himself.

- Have fun talking about the sounds and pictures together – what repeated sound can your child hear in each story?

- Help him break new words into separate sounds (eg. sh-ou-t) and blend their sounds together to say the word.

- Point out how words with the same written ending sound the same. If d-own says 'down', what does he think br-own or cl-own might say?

Books in the phonics series

Book 1 Alphapets
Introduces the most common sound made by each letter, and the capital and small letter shapes.

Book 2 Splat cat
Simple words including the short vowel sounds `a` `e` and `i` as in cat, hen and pig.

Book 3 Hot fox
Simple words including the short vowel sounds `o` and `u` ; simple words including `ch` `sh` or `th`.

Book 4 Stunt Duck
Simple words including the common consonant combinations `ck` `ll` `ss` and `ng`.

Book 5 Sheriff Showoff
More words including common consonant blends: `ff` `st` `mp` `lp` `nch` `nd` and `fl`.

Book 6 Frank's frock
More words including common consonant blends: `fr` `nk` `cl` `tr` `gr` and `nt`.

Match the sounds game

36 self-checking phonic gamecards. Great fun, and the idea way to practise the spellings and so introduced in the phonics storyb

○ Some common words, such as 'sure', 'love' and even 'the', can't be read by sounding out. Help your child practise recognising words like these so that he can read them on sight, as whole words.

Phonic fun

Playing word games with your child is a fun way to build his phonic skills. Try playing rhyming I-Spy, using oy, ow or ar words. Or challenge him to think of as many words with a particular sound in as he can in a minute.

The text applies equally to girls and boys, but the child is referred to as 'he' throughout to avoid the use of the clumsy 'he/she'.